ROB BELL

DROPS LIKE STARS

I KNOW A MAN WHO

HAS TWO SONS.

Both of his sons are married, and both their wives became pregnant in the same year. Out of the two pregnancies,

ONE ENDED IN
A MISCARRIAGE,

THE OTHER IN A
HEALTHY BABY BOY.

And so twice in that year this man I know went to the same hospital, walked down the same hallways with his same family members. The first time to grieve and mourn, the second time to rejoice and celebrate.

WE LIVE IN THE
HALLWAYS, DON'T WE?

In the hallways. We've left one room and gone to the other.
We've sat outside, waiting. We've felt that kind of pain and been
overwhelmed by that kind of joy. We've all been in the hallways
in one way or another, haven't we?

Maybe not in
the same family,
in the same hospital,
in the same hallways,
but this man
with two sons –
we know his story,

BECAUSE HIS STORY
IS OUR STORY.

Jesus told a story about a man who had two sons. The story
begins with the younger son asking for his share of the inheritance,
which in first-century Jewish culture was a deeply offensive request,
the equivalent of saying,

"DAD, I WISH YOU
WERE DEAD."

What an odd way to begin a story.

What's even more unusual is that the father grants his request. The son
leaves with the money and eventually spends it all. In his humiliation
and poverty, the son decides to head home, where he hopes to get work
as one of his father's servants.

But when he arrives home, he isn't shunned or punished or treated as
a servant. His father rushes out to welcome and embrace him and then
throws a party for him. Normally, on an occasion like this, a lamb would
be sacrificed for the meal, which would be enough for a family.

But the father in this story has a calf prepared, which would be enough
for the whole village.

Apparently, the consequences of the son's departure were so
destructive that he needed to be reconciled to the whole community.

This celebration infuriates the older brother. He refuses to join the party
and instead argues the injustice of it all to their father, who responds,

"My son, you are always with me, and everything I have is yours. But we had to celebrate and be glad because this brother of yours was dead and is alive; he was lost and is found."

The older brother then has a moment of profound enlightenment.
He puts his arm around his father and says, "You're right, Dad. I'm sorry I've been such an ass. Can I get you a beer?"

Uh ... actually, that's not how the story ends. The story ends with the father's words about how everything he has belongs to his son and how they have to celebrate because his son "was dead and is alive again."

That's it.

That's how the story ends.
The father's words hanging in the air ...
And we never learn what the elder brother decides to do.

WHAT AN ODD WAY
TO END A STORY.

If this story was a film, it would end with the father's words,
and then the camera would pan back, showing the party
in the background. You'd hear the clinking of silverware and
laughter and the thump of the bass drum on the dance floor
and then the screen would fade to black and the credits would roll.

JESUS LEAVES
THE STORY
UNRESOLVED.

We never find out what the older brother decides to do.

P 13

Jesus doesn't give the story the proper Hollywood ending we've all come to expect.

You can picture one more scene, can't you?

The older brother enters the party and the younger brother is surrounded by people who want to talk to him but he sees his brother and so he says to them "just a minute, please" as he starts walking toward his brother and the orchestra music in the background gets louder and louder as they get closer and closer until they embrace and everybody at the party circles around them and starts clapping and then the camera pans over to that one last shot – the one of the father holding a glass of champagne with a smile on his face and a tear in his eye.

BUT THAT'S NOT
HOW IT ALWAYS
GOES, IS IT?

Some elder brothers never join the party.
Some fathers never throw one.
Some brothers never come back.
Some things never get resolved.

LOTS OF PARTIES ARE MISSING SOMEBODY.

And when we try to resolve things too quickly or pretend that everyone is there when they aren't or offer hollow, superficial explanations ... it's not honest and it's not right and it's not real.
It's not how life is.

I've heard people trying to be helpful in the midst of a tragedy or accident or death by saying, "That's just how God planned it," while I'm thinking, "The god who planned THAT is not a god I want anything to do with."

Others with far more wisdom and experience than me have tackled the "why" questions of suffering.

Here, in these pages, I'm interested in another question ...

NOT "WHY THIS?"
BUT "WHAT NOW?"

This is a standard question on undergrad applications:

"In order for the admissions staff of our college to get to know you, the applicant, better, we ask that you answer the following question: Are there any significant experiences you have had, or accomplishments you have realized, that have helped to define you as a person?"

An applicant named Hugh Gallagher sent this response to NYU:

"I am a dynamic figure, often seen scaling walls and crushing ice. I've been known to remodel train stations on my lunch breaks, making them more efficient in the area of heat retention. I translate ethnic slurs for Cuban refugees. I write award-winning operas. I manage time efficiently. Occasionally, I tread water for three days in a row.

I woo women with my sensuous and godlike trombone playing, I can pilot bicycles up severe inclines with unflagging speed, and I cook Thirty-Minute Brownies in twenty minutes. I am an expert in stucco, a veteran in love, and an outlaw in Peru.

Using only a hoe and a large glass of water, I once single-handedly defended a small village in the Amazon Basin from a horde of ferocious army ants. I play bluegrass cello, I was scouted by the Mets, I am the subject of numerous documentaries. When I'm bored, I build large suspension bridges in my yard. I enjoy urban hang gliding. On Wednesdays, after school, I repair electrical appliances free of charge.

I am an abstract artist, a concrete analyst, and a ruthless bookie. Critics worldwide swoon over my original line of corduroy evening wear.

I don't perspire. I am a private citizen, yet I receive fan mail. I have been caller number nine and have won the weekend passes. Last summer I toured New Jersey with a traveling centrifugal-force demonstration.

I bat .400.

My deft floral arrangements have earned me fame in international botany circles. Children trust me.

I can hurl tennis rackets at small moving objects with deadly accuracy.

I once read *Paradise Lost*, *Moby Dick*, and *David Copperfield* in one day and still had time to refurbish an entire dining room that evening. I know the exact location of every food item in the supermarket. I have performed several covert operations with the CIA. I sleep once a week; when I do sleep, I sleep in a chair.

While on vacation in Canada, I successfully negotiated with a group of terrorists who had seized a small bakery. The laws of physics do not apply to me.

I balance, I weave, I dodge, I frolic, and my bills are all paid.
On weekends, to let off steam, I participate in full-contact origami.

Years ago I discovered the meaning of life but forgot to write it down.
I have made extraordinary four-course meals using only a mouli and a toaster oven.

I breed prizewinning clams. I have won bullfights in San Juan,
cliff-diving competitions in Sri Lanka, and spelling bees at the Kremlin.

I have played Hamlet, I have performed open-heart surgery,
and I have spoken with Elvis.

But I have not yet gone to college."

Brilliant, isn't it? What is it that makes the essay so ... enjoyable? Clearly the content is striking itself – it's weird and smart and imaginative (full contact origami?) and random (touring New Jersey with a traveling centrifugal-force demonstration?) and oddly poetic all at once.

But it isn't just about the "what" – the content; it's also about the "where." It's on a college application, which is generally where people are at their most serious, trying to impress the admissions staff with their eloquence and achievement, not boasting of how they "woo women" with their "sensuous and godlike trombone playing."

There's a phrase we use when we're describing something we consider new and fresh and unexpected.

We say it's "out of the box."

The problem with the phrase is that when something or someone is judged to be in or out of "the box," it reveals that "the box" is still our primary point of reference. We're still operating within the prescribed boundaries and assumptions of how things are supposed to be.

"Out of the box" is sometimes merely another way of being "in the box."

And then there are those, like this applicant, who come from a totally different place.

They ask another kind of question:

"THERE'S A BOX?"

In 1941, in a village in Nazi-controlled Poland, a young man came home to discover that his father had died while he was at work. What made his father's death exceedingly more unbearable was that several years earlier, both this young man's sister and mother had died. As he held his father's dead body in his arms, he lamented,

"I'M ALL ALONE.

At twenty, I've already lost all the people I've loved."

One writer described it like this:

"Ripped out of the soil of his background, his life could no longer be what it used to be. He now began a journey to deeper communion with God.

But it didn't come without tears, and it didn't come without what seems to have been a certain existential horror."

Suffering can do that to us. We're jolted, kicked, prodded, and shoved into new realities we never would have brought about on our own. We're forced to imagine a new future because the one we were planning on is gone.

The key word here is, of course, "imagine."

That young Polish man sitting on the floor with his dead father in his arms was having all of his boxes smashed to pieces.

"HIS LIFE COULD NO LONGER BE WHAT IT USED TO BE."

Now for a multiple choice question:

If we went to a performing arts center on a Saturday night and as we walked in we noticed that everybody was dressed up and backstage there were various performers pacing back and forth in tights and slippers and they had Russian last names, we would know we were at

A. The rodeo
B. An insurance convention
C. The grand opening of a new hair salon
D. The ballet

The location and time and clothes of this event are what art theorists call "insulators." Insulators frame an event, providing context and helping determine the meaning of an experience for us.

If we went to the ballet and everybody in the audience was wearing snorkels or the musicians were all red-haired banjo players with no teeth or instead of being handed a program we were handed a squirrel, we would immediately begin asking,

WHAT IS THIS?

But our real question would be, Where is this? Where do we put this? How do we place it? Because our standard reference points – the usual insulators – wouldn't be there to guide us.

That's often what happens when we suffer. We had things well planned out. We knew what meant what. We had all of our boxes properly organized and labeled. But all of that was disrupted when we began to suffer.

So there's "out of the box," which is often merely a variation of the same thing. And then there are those who think and feel and live and create from a different place. They've had their boxes smashed and their insulators dismantled until they had no other option but to imagine a totally new tomorrow.

WE COULD CALL THIS THE ART OF DISRUPTION.

Hugh Gallagher, of course, was accepted to NYU. And that young Polish man? His name was Karol Jozel Wojtyla, but later in life he was known as Pope John Paul II.

CATHERINE OF
ARAGON SAID,

"NONE GET TO GOD BUT THROUGH TROUBLE."

I live near a village that has several restaurants and a coffee shop and a grocery store and a dry cleaner and a clothing boutique. The main street that runs through the village dead-ends at a yacht club, which is on a lake that has a park at one end with a brick path so that you can walk along the water.

On a warm spring day you can sit on one of the benches along the main street of the village and occasionally a white boy will drive by in his mother's SUV with the windows down. As he passes by, you can hear quite clearly that he's listening to rap – and you can even sometimes pick out the lyrics to the song if he has the stereo in his mother's SUV turned up loud enough.

The song is by a young African-American rapper from an under-resourced, violent neighborhood in a large American city. His lyrics describe in vivid detail what it was like to grow up without a father, struggling just to survive in an environment where the odds were overwhelmingly high that he would end up dealing drugs, doing time in prison, or dead.

Now some of the conditions this rapper is describing in his song are actually happening about three miles west of where this white boy in his mother's SUV lives. But if he was taken there and shown what it actually looks and feels and tastes like in flesh and blood, he would run – or drive – home as fast as he possibly could.

This boy's parents have worked very hard and made significant sacrifices to create an environment in which he will never have to endure the very threats and events the song speaks of.

So why, out of all the songs in the world, does this particular boy choose to play this particular song on the stereo of his mother's SUV?

3 MILES

In the movie *Old School*, Will Ferrell plays a married, thirty-something-year-old suburban man who finds himself at a college party.

When he's offered a drink, he declines, saying,
"I have a big day tomorrow."

When he's asked, "Doing what?" he responds, "Well, um ... actually a pretty nice little Saturday. We're gonna go to Home Depot, buy some wallpaper, maybe get some flooring, stuff like that. Maybe Bed Bath and Beyond ... I don't know. I don't know if we'll have enough time ..."

Why is it that everyone I know who's seen that movie remembers that scene? Obviously people remember it because it's funny. But there's far more going on in the scene than just going to Home Depot on a Saturday.

This man in this movie is bored.

He has the life that is often portrayed as the ideal – a wife, a house, a job, security, comfort, privilege, freedom – and yet it's left him bored, numb, and in a low-grade state of despair. His "success" has actually served to distract him from just how deeply unsatisfied he is with his life.

I assume none of us want to starve or be shot at or lose someone we love, but it's possible to die a sort of death at the other end of the spectrum as well, isn't it?

If we aren't careful, our success and security and abundance can lead to a certain sort of boredom, a numbing predictability, a paralyzing indifference that comes from being too comfortable.

Death by wallpaper and flooring.

In his memoir *What I Talk about When I Talk about Running*, the Japanese writer Haruki Murakami reflects on why runners spend so much time and energy on long distance runs: "It's precisely because of the pain, precisely because we want to overcome that pain, that we can get a feeling, through this process, of really being alive."

IS THIS WHY THE WHITE BOY IN HIS MOTHER'S SUV LISTENS TO THAT SONG?

He wants to feel like he's "really being alive," like he's in the game, like important things are on the line and it's up to him to make a difference. But his world is too comfortable for him, too insulated, and it's making him numb. He may not articulate it this way, but at least when you struggle, you're feeling something. And if he can't have it in real life, then he'll at least get to experience it vicariously through the song that's playing on the stereo of his mother's SUV.

Have you ever gotten angry enough in a conversation to say, "Do you want to know how I really feel?" The moment we say something like that, we reveal that up until that moment, we weren't being entirely truthful. Now obviously, there may have been good reason – knowing when and where to say what and how much is important.

But sometimes there's a truth just below the surface that is, in fact, the real issue. And to get it out in the open, to talk about what really needs to be talked about, to stop pretending and posing and acting, we have to suffer.

Pain has a way of making us more honest.

I know a family whose son committed suicide. He was taken to the hospital, where he laid on life support for several days, brain-dead but breathing – barely.

His eleven-year-old cousin came to the hospital to see him before the machines were turned off. When she got to the room, she told everyone to leave her alone with him. When they got out in the hall and closed the door, they could hear her through the wall, yelling at him: "Why did you do this? I'm so angry with you! Why did you do this?"

She said what everybody wanted to say. She did what they all wanted to do.

THIS IS THE ART
OF HONESTY.

The writer Frederick Beuchner remembers a time in his life when he
was a "twentyseven-year-old bachelor." "[I was] trying to write a novel,
which for one reason or another refused to come to life for me, partly,
I suspect, because I was trying too hard and hadn't learned yet the
importance of letting the empty place inside of me open up."

And so we're polite and we play by the rules and when asked how we are,
we answer, "I'm fine, thank you," just like we're supposed to.

And then we suffer.
There's a disruption
and our boxes get smashed
and the insulators are removed
and the pretense is shattered
and the "empty place" inside of us opens up.

ONLY IF YOU MEAN IT.

This would make an excellent mantra, wouldn't it?

Like an angry eleven-year-old girl, yelling at her hours-from-officially-dead cousin,"Why would you do this?"

Which is the question everybodywanted to yell at him.

Do you know that feeling in class when somebody raises his hand and says, "I don't get it," and you feel so relieved that you aren't the only one who isn't getting it?

That's what great artists do.
This is what great people do.
They ask it.
They say it.
They express it.
They put in words what so many
others are thinking and feeling
and wondering. They affirm that ...

YOU AREN'T THE
ONLY ONE HAVING
THIS EXPERIENCE.

Richard Ashcroft sings a line in the song "Bitter Sweet Symphony":

"I NEED TO HEAR SOME SONGS THAT RECOGNIZE THE PAIN IN ME."

Is this why certain songs move us like they do? Take slave spirituals –
a song like "Sometimes I Feel Like a Motherless Child," which starts
by repeating that line three times and then the line "a long way
from home."

Like me, you've probably never been owned by someone else as a slave.
And yet we hear a song like "Sometimes I Feel Like a Motherless Child"
and we connect with it at some primal level of the soul – even if we've
known our mothers our whole lives.

We're drawn to it because so much of the time

WE'RE SURROUNDED
BY BUZZ
AND GLOSS
AND HYPE –

we slide down the surface of things .

And then we hear something born of suffering and adversity and we're moved because it's honest. It's real. It means something.

IT'S THE ART
OF THE ACHE.

The ache is universal. The ache reminds us that things aren't how they're supposed to be. The ache cuts through all the static, all of the ways we avoid having to actually feel things. The ache reassures us that we're not the only ones who feel this way.

Last year I sprained my hand – my left hand, which is the hand I write with.

So for a while I tried

to write with my right hand

... but that didn't last long.

Now normally I see somebody with their arm in a sling or their wrist in a cast and it barely registers. But the moment I have even the slightest trouble tying my shoes or typing or buttoning my shirt, I'm instantly reminded of all sorts of people I know who have physical limitations – limitations I don't ordinarily even notice.

And a sprained wrist is nothing. It's a momentary inconvenience compared with what lots of people live with their entire lives.

In those moments trying to zip up my jacket,

I FEEL A STRONG SORT OF CONNECTION, SOLIDARITY, EMPATHY.

Just a taste of their every day connects me to them in a mysterious sort of way.

THIS IS A BUMPER STICKER I SEE AROUND WHERE I LIVE.

PRAY FOR JOSH
www.greenhouseministries.org

WHO IS JOSH?

In 2007, Josh Buck was on vacation in Mexico with his family when he was injured in a swimming accident. His neck was fractured, his spinal cord damaged, and he went into a coma.

He survived and has been in a wheelchair ever since.

Two years before his accident, Josh and his wife had a young daughter who died in a freak household accident.

How much pain can one young family endure?

People heard their story and were moved. Not just emotionally moved, as in "I'm so sorry this has happened," but moved to do something.

People brought meals, organized prayer vigils, a group even got together and built them a wheelchair-friendly house.

Yes, an entire house. And, of course, people made bumper stickers.

Imagine being at a public event like a movie or game or play or religious service and before it starts, someone says to the crowd, "Please stand if you've been affected by cancer."

What would you feel?
Compassion?
Empathy?
Solidarity?
Connection?
Love?

A setting of strangers and yet you mention cancer – a specific suffering – and there's instantly a bond.

If someone said,

"Please stand ... if you've been to Hawaii" or
"Please stand ... if you've had to fire your interior decorator" or
"Please stand ... if you drive a station wagon,"

It just wouldn't have the same effect, would it?

BUT SUFFERING, SUFFERING UNITES.

It doesn't matter if you're rich or poor or
black or white or right or left or young or old –
if you have the same disease as someone else
or if you both have a daughter with an eating disorder
or have a brother in jail or had a spouse die
or recently were fired ...

you have a bond that transcends
whatever differences you have.

That's what suffering does.

THIS IS THE ART OF SOLIDARITY.

Is this why people wear crosses around their necks?

The first Christians insisted that when Jesus died on the cross,
this wasn't just another execution by the Roman Empire.

They believed this was the divine,
in flesh and blood,
hanging there on the cross,
bloody, thirsty,
suffering.

A god who is not somewhere else –
remote,
detached,
distant –
but among us,
feeling what we feel,
aching how we ache,

SUFFERING LIKE US.

In the last novel of Susan Howatch's Starbridge series, the confident, self-righteous Bishop Charles Ashworth finds his boxes smashed and insulators destroyed when his beloved wife, Lyle, dies. He ends up in a conversation with an old acquaintance who can't get over how vulnerable and honest the bishop is being with him.

"God, isn't life bloody sometimes!"

"Yes."

"Are you just saying that to be nice to me?"

"No."

"Thank God. Lord, this is a damned odd conversation to be having with a bishop! Excuse me while I just pinch myself to make sure I'm not dreaming."

"It's no dream. Good to meet someone else who's gone through hell lately."

"Isn't it wonderful? It makes all the difference to know there's someone else screaming alongside you – and that's the point of the incarnation. I can see that so clearly now. God came into the world and screamed alongside us. Interesting idea, that."

Perhaps that's why people across the religious spectrum, for thousands of years, continue to identify with the cross. It speaks to our longing to know that we're not alone, that there's someone else "screaming alongside us."

Is the cross God's way of saying, "I know how you feel"?

By the early '90s, the legendary singer Johnny Cash had been all but forgotten by the music industry.

This bothered the music producer Rick Rubin, who suggested they work together. Rubin set up a microphone and asked Johnny Cash to play the guitar and sing whatever songs he wanted to.

A MAN, A GUITAR, AND A MICROPHONE.

After doing this for awhile, Rubin suggested that Johnny Cash play a solo acoustic show at The Viper Room in Los Angeles – a solo acoustic show. Just him and his guitar, all alone on the stage – without his band to back him up like they'd done for years.

Rubin recalled in an interview, "I remember he was terrified before going on. This was a guy who did 200 shows a year for forty years. He'd played in prisons. And the idea of going up by himself, with a guitar and singing songs, absolutely terrified him. I remember watching him, how nervous he was through the first song ... you could hear a pin drop – dead silence."

And in the terror, Johnny Cash found a whole new career. Rick Rubin stripped away the other instruments and musicians and staging and trappings that Johnny Cash had learned to rely on over the years. And in the process, discovered a voice that had been there all along.

Rubin reflected later, "People who were there that night still talk about it as

ONE OF THE
GREATEST THINGS
THEY'VE EVER SEEN."

ROOM

NO
PERSONS
UNDER
21
ALLOWED

THIS IS THE ART OF

ELIMINATION.

Great artists know that it isn't just about what you add; sometimes the most important work is knowing what to take away.

Removing clutter, excess, all the superfluous elements – and finding out in the process what's been in there the whole time.

In *Lust for Life*, Irving Stone's novel about the life of Van Gogh, Van Gogh studies the work of a painter named Bosboom, whose "values were precise and exquisite and Vincent learned that it is always the simplest piece of art which has practiced the most rigid elimination and is, therefore, the most difficult to reproduce."

Mark Twain said that if he'd had more time, he would have said less.

Michaelangelo said that

HIS DAVID WAS IN THE STONE CLAMORING TO BE FREED.

This is the power of the Nike swoosh.
Nike doesn't even have to use its
name for you to know who it is.

It's that simple.

THIS IS A BAR OF SOAP.

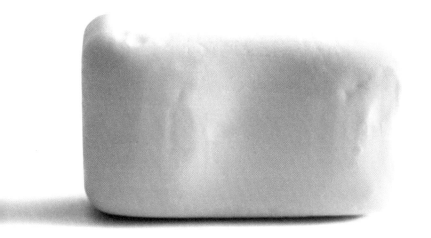

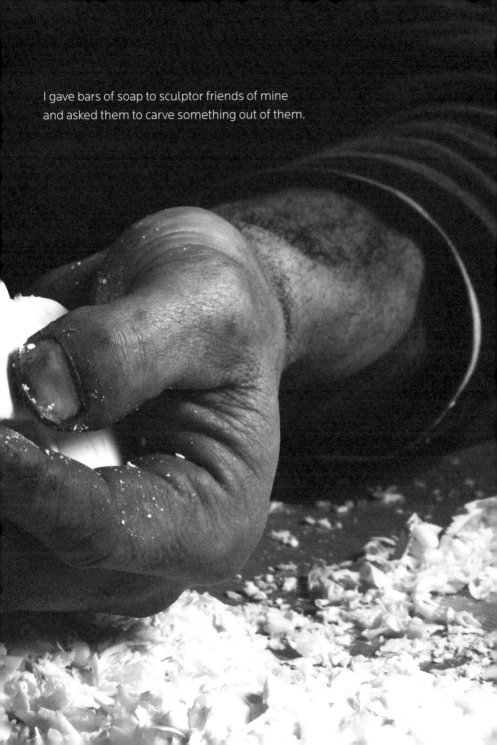

I gave bars of soap to sculptor friends of mine
and asked them to carve something out of them.

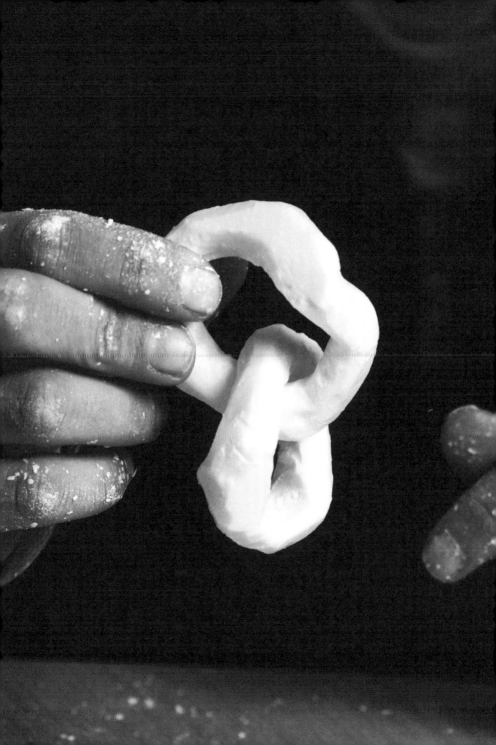

STUNNING, ISN'T IT?

And yet these sculptures were in those bars the whole time. All these sculptors really did was remove.

Sculptors shape and form and rearrange, but at the most basic level they take away. And there is an extraordinary, beautiful art to knowing what to take away.

When you talk with people who have just received news
that they have a life-threatening illness, what do they say?

"Now I must get those hedges trimmed!"

"I've been putting that plastic surgery off long enough."

"It's finally time to join that online poker club."

No, of course not.
They talk about family and friends.
They gather those they love as close as possible.
They reflect on any amends that need to be made with anybody.

They talk about what matters most.

Suffering does that.

IT COMPELS US
TO ELIMINATE
THE UNNECESSARY,
THE TRIVIAL,
THE SUPERFICIAL.

There is greatness in you. Courage. Desire. Integrity. Virtue. Compassion. Dignity. Loyalty. Love.

It's in there – somewhere.

And sometimes it takes suffering to get at it.

It's in there.

This is a Jeff Condon painting that we have hanging in our house. Soon after we put it up, a friend of ours came over, saw it, and said,

"THAT'S A JEFF CONDON!"

She then began raving about what a great artist Jeff Condon is, pointed out the unique perspective of the piece and the way he uses color and the common themes between our painting and other works of his she had seen.

This is one of my guitars. It's a Rickenbacker 330 six-string semi-hollow body with the jet glo finish. I play a little and I can make a fair bit of noise. But my friend Joey? He comes over and starts playing my guitar and evokes sounds out of it I simply cannot.

There is a difference between ownership and possession.

I own the guitar, but Joey possesses it in ways I can't. We own the Jeff Condon painting, but our friend possessed it in ways we don't.

YOU CAN OWN SOMETHING AND NOT POSSESS IT.

YOU CAN POSSESS SOMETHING AND NOT OWN IT.

One of the first Christians, a man named Paul, wrote about his "troubles, hardships, distress, beatings, imprisonment, riots, sleepless nights, hunger."

This is a man who suffered, yet he doesn't end his list with despair.

Paul claims that he and his friends are "genuine, yet regarded as imposters; known, yet regarded as unknown; dying, and yet they live on; beaten, and yet not killed; sorrowful, yet always rejoicing; poor, yet making many rich; "having nothing, and yet possessing everything."

Several years ago I was in Rwanda meeting with a group of women who have AIDS when I began to hear all sorts of noises coming from next door. At first it sounded like somebody was setting up a drum set and then I started to hear singing. When our meeting was over, around noon, I went over to see what was going on. I came around the corner and found myself in a large room packed with people singing and dancing as if it were the last groove on earth. Hundreds of them – swaying and clapping and moving. When I asked my guide what this was, he replied,

"OH, THEY DO THIS EVERY DAY AT LUNCH."

Having nothing, and yet possessing everything.

David Letterman had the musician Warren Zevon on his show
soon after Zevon found out he had cancer. Letterman asked him,
"From your perspective, do you know something about life ... that
maybe I don't know?"

Warren Zevon answered, "I know how much you're supposed to enjoy
every sandwich."

Sometimes what happens to us when we suffer is that we become open
to the mercy and grace and gratitude and gift and appreciation and joy
that are always around us all the time, even in a sandwich.

A while ago I was visiting Buenos Aires, Argentina, during a massive
economic recession. Riding along in the car when I first got there,
I noticed that quite a few cars had bottles on their roofs. It was explained
to me that when a person wants to sell his car, he doesn't put a sign in
the window; he puts a bottle on the roof. People then see it and knock
on the door of his house and hopefully the sale is made. The reason
so many cars were for sale was because such a large percentage of the
population had lost their jobs, almost everybody was in need of money
just to eat and survive.

The next day our hosts had a party for us. They brought out massive grills for the food and their best wine, and after our feast, someone started to play the piano and they gathered and began to sing.

And what did they sing? Cold unemployed Argentineans sang African-American slave songs, including one called "His Eye Is on the Sparrow."

The first verse starts,

"Why should I feel discouraged,
why should the shadows come,
why should my heart be lonely ..."

And as the song continued, they began singing louder and louder, with so much passion and ache in their voices. This wasn't just a song, this was solidarity, hope – there was life with those people, a real true aching thriving sort of life. I learned that singing those songs, sitting hip to hip because they didn't have heat, you can have all of the things that everybody says you need to be happy and yet actually possess very little.

While others, in the process of losing the few things they do have, are, in fact ...

POSSESSING
EVERYTHING.

David Bayles and Ted Orland in their book *Art and Fear* tell the story
of a ceramics teacher who divided the class into two groups – one group
would be graded on how much they created in the designated time,
while the other group would be graded on the quality of the one work
they made. In the end, it was

THE "QUANTITY"
GROUP THAT ENDED
UP PRODUCING THE
WORKS OF MOST
QUALITY.

They conclude "that while the 'quantity' group was busy churning
out piles of work – and learning from their mistakes – the 'quality' group
had sat theorizing about perfection, and in the end had little more to
show for their efforts than grandiose theories and a pile of dead clay."

This isn't true just for ceramics students.

When I'm meeting with my counselor and I use words like "mistake"
or "failure" or "waste," he stops me.

He then reaches into his desk drawer and pulls out a sign and holds
it up so I can read it – again.

Now it's absolutely necessary for us to own and name and claim and make amends for our failures and mistakes and sins and wrongs where others are concerned.

But to stop there is tragic.

It isn't just a failure, a mistake, a sin, a wrong ...

IT'S ALSO AN
OPPORTUNITY

to grow, expand, evolve, learn.

This is called the art of failure. What every artist must learn is that even the failed pieces are essential. The Franciscan priest Richard Rohr points out that Native Americans have a tradition of leaving a blemish in one corner of the rug they are weaving

BECAUSE THEY
BELIEVE THAT'S WHERE
THE SPIRIT ENTERS.

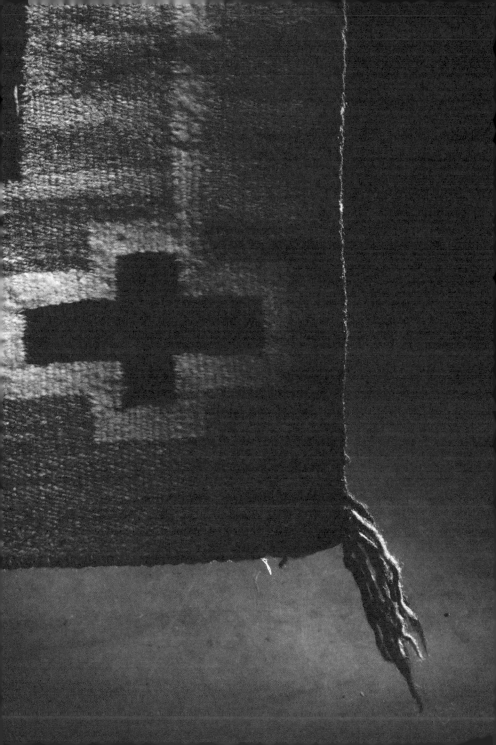

I can relate to the rugs.

I want desperately for things to go "how they're supposed to."
Which is another way of saying "how I want them to," which
is another way of saying "according to my plan."

And that, as we all know, isn't how it works.

But it's in that disappointment, in that confusion, in that pain – the
pain that comes from things not going how I wanted them to – that I find
the same thing happening, again and again. I come to the end of myself,
to the end of my power, the end of my strength, the end of my
understanding, only to find in that place of powerlessness
a strength and peace that weren't there before.

I keep discovering that it's in the blemish that the Spirit enters.

The cross, it turns out, is about the mysterious work of God which
begins not with big plans and carefully laid out timetables

BUT IN PAIN
AND ANGUISH
AND DEATH.

It's there, in the agony of those moments, that we get the first glimpses of just what it looks like for God to take all of our trauma and hurt and disappointment, all those fragments lying there on the ground, and turn them into something else, something new, something we never would have been able to create on our own.

It's in that place that we're reminded that true life comes when we're willing to admit that we've reached the end of ourselves, we've given up, we've let go, we're willing to die to all of our desires to figure it out and be in control.

WE LOSE OUR LIFE, ONLY TO FIND IT.

It turns out that a Navajo rug and a Roman cross have a lot in common.

We are going to suffer.
And it is going to shape us.
Somehow.

We will become

OR BETTER

CLOSED

OR OPEN

MORE IGNORANT

OR MORE AWARE

MORE

OR LESS

tuned in to the thousands
upon thousands of gifts we
are surrounded with every single
moment of every single day.

This too will shape me.
The only question left is, how?

Just before he died in 1972, Abraham Joshua Heschel was asked in an interview if he had anything to say to young people. This was his answer: "Above all, remember that the meaning of life is to

LIVE IT AS IF IT WERE A WORK OF ART.

YOU'RE NOT A MACHINE.

When you're young, start working on this great work of art called your own existence."

Heschel's words remind me of the perspective the sculptor Harriet March gives in one of Susan Howatch's novels. When a theologian comes to visit her at her studio and he has all sorts of polished and complicated ideas about God and suffering and life, Harriet explains to him how she sees the world through her work.

"But no matter how much the mess and distortion make you want to despair, you can't abandon the work because you're chained to the bloody thing, it's absolutely woven into your soul and you know you can never rest until you've brought truth out of all the distortion and beauty out of all the mess – but it's agony, agony, agony – while simultaneously being the most wonderful and rewarding experience in the world – and that's the creative process which so few people understand."

She reminds me of the hallway at the hospital – "agony, agony, agony" and yet "simultaneously being the most wonderful and rewarding experience in the world."

She continues, "It involves an indestructible sort of fidelity, an insane sort of hope, and indescribable sort of ... well, it's love, isn't it? There's no other word for it ... And don't throw Mozart at me ... I know he claimed his creative process was no more than a form of automatic writing, but the truth was he sweated and slaved and died young giving birth to all that music. He poured himself out and suffered. That's the way it is. That's creation ... You can't create without waste and mess and sheer undiluted slog. You can't create without pain. It's all part of the process. It's in the nature of things."

Ever felt like that? Like whatever you were going through wasn't just hard or exhausting or difficult but that it was

SHEER UNDILUTED
SLOG?

She doesn't give us any answers, she doesn't tell us why making things is like that, she simply says that the point is to stay true to whatever it is you're creating.

And then she finishes with these magnificent words:

"So in the end every major disaster, every tiny error, every wrong turning, every fragment of discarded clay, all the blood, sweat and tears – everything has meaning. I give it meaning. I reuse, reshape, recast all that goes wrong so that in the end nothing is wasted and nothing is without significance and nothing ceases to be precious to me."

At the end of her speech, I have a question: is she talking about sculpture or life? My hope is that by the end of this book, your answer to that question will be yes.

Several years ago, my three-year-old nephew and I were standing in front of a large window, watching it rain. He started saying,

"STARS, STARS, STARS."

I turned to my sister-in-law and asked, "Why does he keep repeating 'stars, stars, stars'?" She answered, "He thinks that when raindrops hit the ground, for a split second they look like stars."

I'D NEVER SEEN
IT THAT WAY.

MAY YOU SEE

DROPS LIKE STARS.

ZONDERVAN

Drops Like Stars
Copyright © 2009 by Rob Bell

Requests for information should be addressed to:

Zondervan, *Grand Rapids, Michigan 49530*

This edition: ISBN: 978-0-310-32704-2 (softcover)

Library of Congress Cataloging-in-Publication Data

Bell, Rob.
    Drops like stars : a few thoughts on creativity and suffering / Rob Bell.
      p. cm.
    ISBN 978-0-310-27503-9 (hardcover)
    1. Suffering—Religious aspects—Christianity. 2. Creation (Literary, artistic, etc.)—
Religious aspects—Christianity. I. Title.
    BV4909.B46 2009
    242'.4—dc22   2009021679

Published in association with Yates & Yates, www.yates2.com

Book design by Mark Baas (BaasCreative.com) and Seth Herman

Printed in China

10 11 12 13 14 15 /CTC/ 23 22 21 20 19 18 17 16 15 14 13 12 11 10 9 8 7 6 5 4 3 2 1

ENDNOTES

P 10   For more perspectives on Jesus' story of two sons, which is found in the Bible in the book of Luke, chapter 15, see *The Prodigal God* by Timothy Keller (New York: Dutton, 2008), *Poet and Peasant* by Kenneth Bailey (Grand Rapids: Eerdmans, 1976), and *The Return of the Prodigal Son* by Henri Nouwen (New York: Doubleday, 1992).

P 20   Hugh Gallagher's "3A Essay" is printed with permission from the author. Find out more at www.hughgallagher.net.

P 24   See Karol Jozef Wojtyla's lament from the book *Pope John Paul II* by Peggy Noonan (New York: Viking, 2005).

P 27   For more about insulators, see *A Year with Swollen Appendices* by Brian Eno (London: Faber and Faber, 1996).

P 39   *Old School* was directed by Todd Phillips (DreamWorks Pictures, 2009).

P 42   Haruki Murakami, *What I Talk about When I Talk about Running* (New York: Knopf, 2008).

P 44   Frederick Buechner's quote is from *Secrets in the Dark* (New York: HarperCollins, 2006).

P 48   "Bitter Sweet Symphony" can be found on The Verve's *Urban Hymns* (Virgin Records, 1998).

P 71   Quote is from *Absolute Truths* by Susan Howatch (New York: Knopf, 1995), the sixth novel in her Starbridge series.

P 72   Interview excerpts are taken from the articles "Rick Rubin on Cash's Legacy" by David Fricke in *Rolling Stone* (September 23, 2003) and "Meet Me in Heaven: The Final Years of Johnny Cash" by Adam D. Miller in *Being There Magazine* (www.beingtheremag.com).

P 78   Quote is from *Lust for Life* by Irving Stone (New York: Plume, 1984).

P 95   See www.jeffcondonart.com.

P 101   Quote is from the Bible in the book of 2 Corinthians, chapter 6.

P 102   Warren Zevon was interviewed on the *Late Show with David Letterman* on October 30, 2002 (show #1895).

P 104   Lyrics of "His Eye Is on the Sparrow" were written by Civilla Martin in 1905.

P 106   The ceramics class story and insight are from *Art and Fear* by David Bayles and Ted Orland (Santa Barbara: Capra Press, 1993), 29.

P 122   Abraham Joshua Heschel gave this answer in an interview by Carl Stern for NBC in 1972.

P 122   Harriet the sculptor's speech is from *Absolute Truths* by Susan Howatch (New York: Knopf, 1995), the sixth novel in her Starbridge series.

THANKS FROM ROB BELL

I read the handwritten first version of this book out loud to my friend Mark Baas, who also happens to be quite a smashing designer. When I finished reading he said, "I'll do whatever it takes to make this book." And so he did. As creative director of the book, Mark gathered together the equally committed Jay Irwin for photography and Seth Herman for design work. With Mark's vision for the book creating all sorts of energy, they worked tirelessly to bring this book into existence. To them I am grateful beyond words.

I continue to deeply appreciate the fine folks at Zondervan: John Topliff for his poems and presence, Angela Scheff for her editorial wisdom and unflinching candor, Dudley Delffs for never giving up on this book actually being made, Karen Smith for smiling in meetings and knowing it will all work out, Michelle Lenger and Brian Phipps for their excellence and attention to detail, and Moe Girkins for getting it, again and again.

Special mention goes out to Randy Bishop, production chief extraordinaire, who went above and beyond, causing us to utter rapturous praise over things like ... paper quality. Many thanks to Hugh Gallagher for graciously allowing the use of his essay, Rick Devos for the aerial photo, Chuck Anderson for wisdom and perspective along the way, Santino Stoner for saving those lunchtime videotapes, Joey Dornbas for playing and posing, and my soap sculpture friends: Carson Brown, Jonathan White, Kevin Buist, Cameron VanDyke, Rachel VanDyke, Rick Beerhorst, Brenda Beerhorst, Taylor Greenfield, and Rick Weese. Lucy Russo, may you run like the wind. Carolyn Baas, let's talk about lettuce wraps. Jon Bell, Mark Tanis, and Matthew Hickman: the gang is now together. Chris Ferebee, we're just getting started.

K, T, P, and V – all my love.

Carolyn, thank you for the inspiration. You are gracious, beautiful, and a joy to be with.

Isabella & Maxwell, thank you for always showing me new ways to see the beauty in our world.

Rob Bell, thank you for writing this book - it continues to inspire me.

Jay Irwin, thank you for your relentless determination to get the work done.

Seth Herman, thank you for all your hard work and for bringing lots of candy.

Mike Smith, thank you for teaching me and investing in me.

Art direction & design: Mark Baas (www.BaasCreative.com)
Design: Seth Herman
Photography: Jay Irwin
Cover retouch: Chuck Anderson
Project management: Carolyn Baas
Project assitance: Lucy Russo
Aerial photo: Rick DeVos
Squirrel photo: Taylor Gahm
Viper Room photo: John Bucher
2nd shooter flower photos: Ryan Prins
Times Square photo: He Shi